∧ Top Notes *Drama Guides*

Tennessee William's

A Streetcar Named Desire

Study notes for American Drama

Nisha Prichard

——A——
FIVE SENSES
PUBLICATION

Five Senses Education Pty Ltd
2/195 Prospect Highway
Seven Hills 2147
New South Wales
Australia

Prichard, Nisha
Top Notes – A Streetcar Named Desire
ISBN 978-1-74130-091-8

TOP NOTES DRAMA SERIES

This series has been created to assist H.S.C. students of Drama in their understanding of set texts. Top Notes are easy to read, providing analysis of issues and discussion of important ideas contained in the texts.

Particular care has been taken to ensure that students are able to examine each text in the context of the module it has been allocated to.

Each text includes:

♦ Notes on the specific module
♦ Plot summary
♦ Character analysis
♦ Setting
♦ Thematic concerns
♦ Language studies
♦ Essay questions and a modelled response
♦ Other textual material
♦ Study practice questions
♦ Useful quotes

I am sure you will find these Top Notes useful in your studies of Drama.

Bruce Pattinson
Series Editor

CONTENTS

THE DRAMA COURSE

The HSC Drama Course is divided into 4 key components

• Australian Drama and Theatre (Core component)
• Studies in Drama and Theatre
• The Group Performance (Core component)
• The Individual Project.

Both the Australian Drama and Theatre and Studies in Drama and Theatre component require the study of specific plays, both as texts and in performance.

In these components you are expected to:

❑ Appreciate the dynamics of drama as an art and a cultural expression

❑ Understand historical and political contexts that have influenced the writing and reception of dramatic texts

❑ Understand the actor-audience relationship

❑ Appreciate the values and issues expressed in drama concerning Australia and other societies

❑ Appreciate the role of the audience in the performance of drama

The study of *A Streetcar Named Desire* is part of The Studies in Drama and Theatre Section in Topic 8:American Drama. Covered in this topic is: "the forms and conventions, the dramatic styles and techniques, performance styles and conventions and the social context of the plays" (NSW Board of Studies Course Prescriptions 2006-2008)

A study includes "The ways in which the plays extend realism through the use of Expressionist and Symbolist techniques and ways in which they might be produced on the contemporary stage" (NSW Board of Studies Course Prescriptions 2006-2008)

All this essentially means is that to do well in this subject you have to know the play *A Streetcar Named Desire* in great detail (both as a dramatic text and as a performance) and understand its ongoing contribution to American drama. These plays are not to be examined the same way you would an English text. It is important to always consider how what is written on the page would actually look like on the stage!

STUDYING A DRAMA TEXT

The medium of any text is very important. If a text is a drama this must not be forgotten. Plays are not *read* they are *viewed*. This means you should never refer to the "reader" but the "audience" as the respondent to the text. The marker will want to know you are aware of the text as a play and that you have considered its effect in performance.

Remembering a drama text is a play also means when you are exploring *how* the composer represents his/her ideas you MUST discuss dramatic techniques. This applies to any response you do using a drama, irrespective of the form the response is required to be in.

Dramatic techniques are all the devices the playwright uses to represent his or her ideas. They are the elements of a drama that are manipulated by playwrights and directors to make any drama effective on stage! You might also see them referred to as dramatic devices or theatrical techniques.

Every play uses dramatic techniques differently. Some playwrights, such as Tennessee Williams are very specific about how they want their play performed on stage. Others like Shakespeare give virtually no directions. They might give detailed comments at the beginning of the play and/or during the script. These are usually in italics and are called *stage directions.* They are never spoken but provide a guide to the director and actors about how the play is to appear and sound when performed.

Some common dramatic techniques are shown on the diagram that follows.

DRAMATIC TECHNIQUES

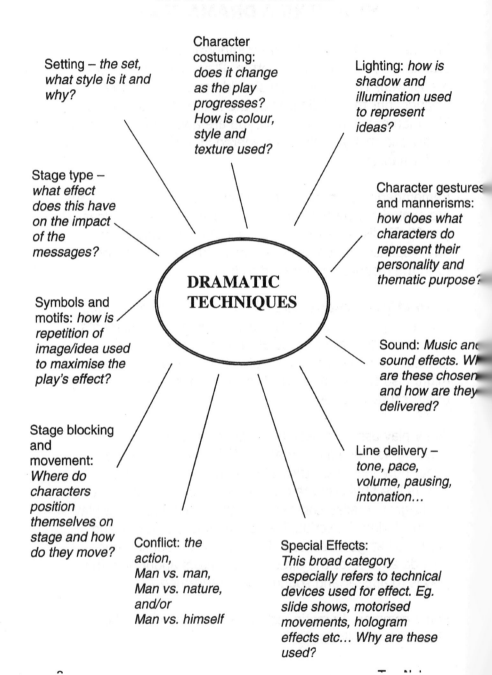

Setting – *the set, what style is it and why?*

Character costuming: *does it change as the play progresses? How is colour, style and texture used?*

Lighting: *how is shadow and illumination used to represent ideas?*

Stage type – *what effect does this have on the impact of the messages?*

Character gestures and mannerisms: *how does what characters do represent their personality and thematic purpose?*

DRAMATIC TECHNIQUES

Symbols and motifs: *how is repetition of image/idea used to maximise the play's effect?*

Sound: *Music and sound effects. What are these chosen and how are they delivered?*

Stage blocking and movement: *Where do characters position themselves on stage and how do they move?*

Line delivery – *tone, pace, volume, pausing, intonation...*

Conflict: *the action, Man vs. man, Man vs. nature, and/or Man vs. himself*

Special Effects: *This broad category especially refers to technical devices used for effect. Eg. slide shows, motorised movements, hologram effects etc... Why are these used?*

8

AMERICAN THEATRE

At the beginning of the twentieth century American theatre was heavily dominated by commercialism. As a reaction to this several amateur groups such as Washington Street Players sprung up in New York City. One of the first key playwrights of the era, Eugene O'Neil emerged from a similar group, -The Provincetown Players. He endlessly searched for a unique theatrical style through his work such as the expressionistic play *Emperor Jones* (1920). He finally found a suitable style in modern tragedy for his autographical play *Long Day's Journey into Night* (1941)

New York City's Theatre Guild established the extremely successful Art theatre in 1918. This was vital to this era because it was built in the grand European tradition audiences were used to and was a dedicated space for amateur American groups. The Guild became an extremely vital platform for American drama by encouraging American playwrights to experiment with their new plays. Combinations of expressionistic, symbolist and realistic techniques gave great psychological depth to the plays and spurned the following of Stanislavsky's Method acting style.

Move forward to the 1940s/50s. Live theatre now had to compete with motion pictures and the beginnings of television. Experimentation was once again needed. More than ever barriers between the audience and performers were deemed restrictive. They needed to see themselves on stage. Tennessee Williams aimed to do that with *A Streetcar Named Desire*. He gave the audiences characters that could have walked straight out of the

French Quarter. The actors that worked on the first productions used method acting to give realistic portrayals. Williams experimented with expressionism and symbols to give outer representation to the characters inner thoughts.

STUDIES IN DRAMA AND THEATRE CONCEPTS

FORM
This is the structure of the play. It helps to distinguish one structure from another

GENRE
Such as comedy, tragedy, farce, melodrama. These dramatic forms can be divided further. For example a comedy may be satirical, absurdist, or romantic.

CONVENTION
An audience makes an agreement to suspend disbelief and accept what appears on stage as reality. The stage itself is a convention-often indoor and outdoor scenes take place on the same three-sided set. Different styles have different conventions. In Japanese Kabuki Theatre a horse is represented with a wooden frame with 4 legs. In English pantomime 2 actors share a horse costume. In Peter Schaeffer's modern drama *Equus*, actors wearing hooves and wire framed headpieces act as horses.

STYLE
Shown in dramatic work by the choices a playwright makes. The techniques employed in a play determine it's style eg kinds of characters, time periods, setting, language, symbols etc

Style changes according to theatrical conventions and traditions and often playwright's may ignore these all together to create their own style. Modern drama tends to be eclectic and blends many styles together.

Theatrical styles can be divided into two categories:

Representational-dialogue, setting, characters, action, are represented as true to life (like realism). Play is stage centred.

Presentational-Actors acknowledge the audience, sometimes speaking directly to them. Aspects are life are presented. Play is audience centred.

The most important concepts you will need to know with regards to American Theatre are Realism, Symbolism and Expressionism. These are very different dramatic styles that 20th Century American playwrights employed.

REALISM

Realism is the use of real (identifiable) people, in real settings, using everyday language. What is most striking about this style is its ordinariness. The focus is on ordinary experiences in American middle class life. The characters are not heroes or villains, but people, who have strengths and weaknesses.

EXPRESSIONISM/SYMBOLISM

A term used widely across all art forms. In theatre it simply means the expression of the playwright's emotions, feelings and attitudes. The stage is no longer like a photograph of life (like realism is); it is more like a painting. In symbolism staging, costumes, lighting, music, scenery become non-realistic and instead represents certain concerns (an underlying meaning to what is on stage). In expressionism they are also used to highlight the protagonist's version of reality. Often expressionistic plays become dream-like with no recognisable plot, conflicts, and character developments. Expressionistic and symbolist techniques can often be used to help illuminate an aspect of a realistic character or theme.

THE PLAYWRIGHT-

TENNESSEE WILLIAMS

Tennessee Williams was born in Columbus, Missouri. His grandfather was a clergyman and his father a travelling salesman. When he was twelve Williams' family moved to St Louis. He and his sister found it difficult to adapt to the city. At aged 16 he won third prize in an essay competition with an essay called 'Can a Good Wife Be a Good Sport?'

During the depression Williams began college. A couple of years later he left and got a clerical job for a shoe company. This lasted for two years. He spent his evenings writing.

In 1938 he entered the University of Iowa. While completing his course he held a variety of different part-time jobs. His play, *Battle of Angels* earned him the Rockerfeller fellowship in 1940.

Near the close of the war in 1944 what many feel is Williams finest play *The Glass Menagerie* was played in Chicago and later Broadway. It was extremely autobiographical. This plays main character-Laura was based on Williams's own extremely ill sister Rose. Most of the violent characters in his plays including *A Streetcar Named Desire's* Stanley were based on Williams often-bombastic father. Homosexuality, Alcoholism, and the fate of his beloved 'Old South' were other aspects of Williams's life that frequently made it into his plays.

Over the next eight years there were continual successful Broadway productions of many of his plays: *A Streetcar Named Desire (1947), Summer and Smoke (1948), A Rose Tattoo (1951), and Camino Real (1953)*. Although his reputation on Broadway continued to grow, particularly upon receiving his first Pulitzer Prize in 1948 for Streetcar, Williams reached a larger worldwide public when *The Glass Menagerie* (1950) and *A Streetcar Named Desire* (1951) were made into motion pictures, following close work with legendary director Elia Kazan (b1909). Williams had now achieved a fame few playwrights of his day could equal.

Williams spent the next phase of his life dividing his time between homes in Key West, New Orleans, and New York, his reputation continued to grow and he saw many more of his works produced on Broadway and made into films, including *Cat on a Hot Tin Roof* (for which he earned a second Pulitzer Prize in 1955), *Orpheus Descending*, and *Night of the Iguana.*

In 1963 Williams lost his long-time companion Frank Merlo, who died of cancer. He was tired of Broadway, and he wanted to do something else. His writing took again an experimental turn. *In the Bar of A Tokyo Hotel* was written in this period and deals with the difficulties of creativity. In 1969 he spent two months on a detoxification program, designed to free him from prolonged dependency on alcohol, amphetamines, and barbiturates.

The 70's saw him gain some control over his life again and he wrote many more plays including:

o *The Red Devil Battery Sign (1976),*

- *Vieux Carré (1977),*
- *A Lovely Sunday For Creve Coeura (1978),*

and his last play

- *Clothes For A Summer Hotel* (1980).

Williams died on February 24, 1983, at the Hotel Elysée in New York City.

HISTORICAL/ SOCIAL CONTEXT

When studying any of the plays for the American Drama unit it is vital to know the context-historical and social of the plays at the time they written. The Playwright is profoundly influenced by what is around them.

CONTEXT OF *A Streetcar Named Desire.*

A Streetcar Named Desire draws from many different interests of Williams. He often wrote from an allusion or adaptation of his own experience. The works of DH Lawrence, the old south he grew up in, his religious background and many different people he encountered in his life were all inspiration. For instance while fictional characters-Mitch and Stanley were the names of two of Williams' college buddies. Many speculate Williams saw himself in both the tragic story of the homosexual Alan Grey, and the faded Southern dame Blanche.

World War Two was a pivotal moment in American history. It is there in the background of this play. Stanley and Mitch both served in the army and it gives a pretty good explanation for a lot of their behaviour, particularly Stanley's aggression.

Following the devastation of WW11 there was a need for a re-building of American culture. In 1947-when Williams wrote *A Streetcar Named Desire* America was just beginning to emerge from two world wars and the Great Depression. The country was becoming a cultural melting pot as migrants from all over the world made America home.

There was a stark contrast between the past and the future. This was especially seen in the southern states. Previously a huge agrarian economy-produced on enormous plantations dominated these areas in particular. Wealth was concentrated in the hands of the aristocratic few. With the introduction of greater technology and the shift towards manufacturing and factory production this world was fast becoming obsolete as more egalitarian and capitalist notions took over.

In *A Streetcar Named Desire* it is clear that Blanche represents the 'old south' and Stanley is the modern, vibrant New Orleans. Williams never states one is necessarily better than the other but he is making a clear statement about what America was like at that particular time.

GLOSSARY

There are some old-fashioned and specifically American terms in *A Streetcar Named Desire.* that might be confusing because they aren't really in use any more. This list should help with understanding them.

Bromo

Pain reliever medicine. Specifically for stomach upsets.

Blue Moon Cocktail

A drink made from Amaretto and Bailey's Irish Cream.

Drug Store

A chemist shop/newsagent that sells refreshments.

Poor boy's sandwich

A sandwich made with beans, onion and bacon. Generally applies to any sandwich made with freshly baked "French Bread", a long, narrow loaf of bread traditional to New Orleans.

Porch

Veranda

Red Hots:

A cinnamon flavoured candy.

Tamales

Spicy Mexican dish using roast pork wrapped in corn shucks (The outside leaves of a corn ear).

PLOT OUTLINE

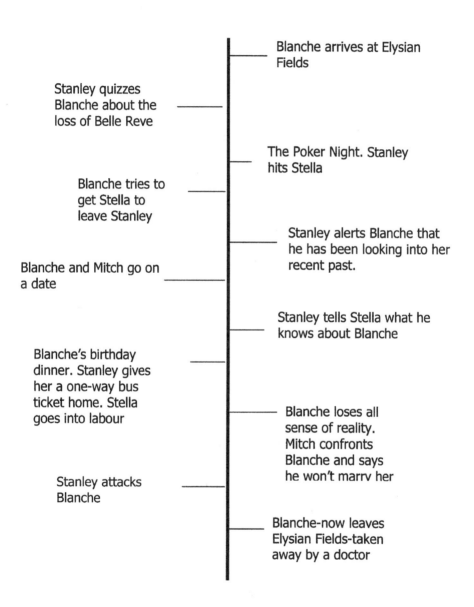

Blanche arrives at Elysian Fields

Stanley quizzes Blanche about the loss of Belle Reve

The Poker Night. Stanley hits Stella

Blanche tries to get Stella to leave Stanley

Stanley alerts Blanche that he has been looking into her recent past.

Blanche and Mitch go on a date

Stanley tells Stella what he knows about Blanche

Blanche's birthday dinner. Stanley gives her a one-way bus ticket home. Stella goes into labour

Blanche loses all sense of reality. Mitch confronts Blanche and says he won't marry her

Stanley attacks Blanche

Blanche-now leaves Elysian Fields-taken away by a doctor

PLOT SUMMARY

SCENE ONE

Blanche arrives in Elysian Fields. She tells her sister Stella of the loss of their family plantation Belle Reve. She is obviously under some strain. She meets Stella's husband Stanley.

SCENE TWO

Stanley is concerned Blanche is trying to swindle Stella (and consequently himself) out of money from the sale of Belle Reve and confronts her about it. She explains how it was gradually lost on mortgages. Stanley tells her Stella is pregnant.

SCENE THREE

Stanley has a poker night. Blanche is introduced to his friend Mitch. Stanley is drunk and enraged by the noise Blanche and Stella are making and hits Stella. Stella races to her neighbour Eunice's place upstairs. Stanley screams for her and she goes back inside with him. Blanche is left outside with Mitch.

SCENE FOUR

Blanche is nearly hysterical at Stella for going back to Stanley. She tries to contact an old beau-Shep Huntley to get money so she and Stella can leave. Stella tries to explain why she won't leave Stanley.

SCENE FIVE

Stanley alerts Blanche that he has been looking into her recent past. Blanche is terrified that Stella now knows some of her bad behaviour. She hopes marrying Mitch may be a solution to her situation. Blanche kisses a young newspaper collector.

SCENE SIX

Blanche and Mitch go on a date. It is extremely awkward and Blanche seems to be keeping a demure distance from him. She tells him the story of her dead husband Alan Grey-her discovery of his homosexuality and his suicide when she confronted him about it.

SCENE SEVEN

It's Blanche's birthday and Stanley tells Stella what he now knows about her many indiscretions and how she was forced to leave her teaching job and town after an affair with a student. Stella tries to defend Blanche but Stanley is determined to tell Mitch everything and get Blanche to leave.

SCENE EIGHT

Stanley, Stella and Blanche have a miserable birthday dinner. Stanley presents Blanche with a one-way bus ticket Stanley tries to reassure Stella things will be fine after she goes. They have an argument and the scene ends with Stella in labour.

SCENE NINE

Blanche is all alone and quickly deteriorating. Mick appears. She makes a desperate attempt to regain his affection, but it is too late-he knows everything. He has a good look at her in full light and is disgusted. He will not marry her .She chases him out of the house.

SCENE TEN

Blanche has completely lost all sense of reality, and is talking to imaginary suitors. Stanley returns home and informs her they will be all alone-Stella is still in hospital. She makes up a story about a cruise with Shep Huntley to escape this but it is futile. Stanley rapes her.

SCENE ELEVEN

It is some time later and another poker game is being played. Blanche has been told she is going to rest in he country but has mistaken that for a trip with Shep Huntley. A doctor and nurse come and take her away as she gratefully accepts, 'the kindness of strangers'. Stella is absolutely distraught but cannot believe Blanche if she, Stanley and their baby boy are to have a future.

SOME USEFUL PLOT QUOTES

SCENE ONE

'They told me take a streetcar named Desire, and then transfer to one called Cemeteries and ride six blocks and get off at-Elysian Fields!'
(Blanche)

'But you are the one that abandoned Belle Reve not I! I stayed and fought for it, bled for it, almost died for it!'
(Blanche)

SCENE TWO

'It looks to me like you've been swindled baby, and when you're swindled under the Napoleonic code I'm swindled *too'*
(Stanley)

'Piece by piece, our improvident grandfathers and father and uncles and brothers exchanged the land for their epic fornications.'
(Blanche)

SCENE THREE

'Poker should not be played in a house with women.'
(Mitch)

'I want my baby down here. Stella, Stella!'
(Stanley)

SCENE FOUR

'But there's things that happen between a man and a woman in the dark-that sort of make everything else-seem-unimportant'
(Stella)

'Maybe he'll strike you or maybe grunt and kiss you! That is if kisses have been discovered yet!
(Blanche)

SCENE FIVE

'Soft people have got to court the favour of hard ones Stella. Have got to be seductive-'
(Blanche)

'It would be nice to keep you, but I've got to be good and keep my hands off children.'
(Blanche)

SCENE SIX

'We danced the Varsouviana! Suddenly in the middle of the dance the boy I had married broke away from me and ran out of the casino. A few moments later-a shot!
(Blanche)

'You need somebody. And I need somebody, too. Could it be-you and me, Blanche?'
(Mitch)

SCENE SEVEN

'Yep, was pratickly a town ordinance passed against her!'
(Stanley)

'I'd have that on my conscience the rest of my life if I knew all that stuff and let my best friend get caught!
(Stanley)

SCENE EIGHT

'Stell, it's gonna be all right after she goes and after you've had the baby.'
(Stanley)

'People like you abused, her and forced her to change'
(Stella)

SCENE NINE

'You're not clean enough to bring in the house with my mother.'
(Mitch)

'I don't mind you being older than I thought. But the rest of it-God!'
(Mitch)

SCENE TEN

'She has decked herself out in a somewhat soiled and crumpled white satin evening gown and a pair of scuffed silver slippers'

'Tiger-tiger! Drop the bottle-top! Drop it! We've had this date with each other from the beginning!'
(Stanley)

SCENE ELEVEN

'I couldn't believe her story and go on living with Stanley.'
(Stella)

'Whoever you are-I have always depended on the kindness of strangers.'
(Blanche)

PLOT QUESTIONS

❏ Trace Blanche's fortunes. At what stage is she doing well, when does she suffer setbacks?

❏ What is the significance of Blanche's story about how Belle Reve was lost?

❏ What purpose do the poker nights serve?

❏ Why does Blanche have her encounter with the 'young man' in scene 5-just after her conversation with Stella?

❏ What do Blanche's references to, and attempts to contact, Shep Huntley suggest about her situation?

❏ Why does Blanche's birthday party occur just as Stanley decides to reveal her secrets?

❑ The play is often viewed as a battle between Blanche and Stanley for the affections of Stella. Trace who is winning at the end of scene 4, at the end of scene eight and at the end of scene 11. Give reasons for their victories

SETTING

The play takes place in the interior of a small apartment in the French Quarter of New Orleans, Louisiana. Williams describes the walls of the apartment as being see-through. This suggests the outside invading the interior-just as Blanche invades the lives of Stanley and Stella and harsh reality eventually overcomes Blanche.

Williams suggests that most houses around here are white framed-but 'weathered grey, with rickety outside stairs and galleries and quaintly ornamented gables to the entrance of both'. However, the actual apartment is not as important to the setting as the atmosphere of the streets and New Orleans. It is vital that the audience comes to understand the kind of world Stella and Stanley inhabit and how Blanche could never fit in there.

New Orleans has always been one of America's most cosmopolitan cities-African Americans and migrants in particular injected their music and culture into the area. Williams tells us that this section is poor but charming. This is represented by the Blue Piano (old piano playing blues type music), which is heard in the background throughout the play. Williams tells us that, *'This Blue Piano' expresses the sprit of life, which goes on here.'*

Various minor characters-The Negro woman, A Mexican woman, Pablo and Stanley's other poker buddies help to convey a sense of what life in the French Quarter is like. In the very first scene we see The Negro woman sharing a rude story with Stanley and Stella's neighbour Eunice.

Clearly everyone in this area is friendly to each other, regardless of race. This is sharp contrast with Blanche and her bigoted notions, expressed when she calls Stanley a 'Polack'.

The apartment is furnished realistically. In each scene the mess of daily life in this area accumulates. Liquor and beer bottles, empty food containers and clothes all fill the stage. The audience senses that this kind of setting is vibrant and chaotic. In scene four Williams offers the following description, 'the table is sloppy with remains of breakfast and the debris of the previous night, and Stanley's gaudy pyjamas lie across the threshold of the bathroom.'

The city is constantly in the background of the play. The trains passing on the nearby L&N tracks, the drums and trumpets from the bars around the corner and cars are heard in the background constantly. Because it would be impossible to put all of this on stage sounds play a vital part in establishing the setting.

The French Quarter is not conveyed purely as an idealistic place. It is quite menacing, especially for Blanche as she soon finds out that she is not really all that welcome there. As the play progresses the noises of the train and the screams from the street no longer seem happy and friendly but almost inhuman. The tiny apartment of Stanley and Stella seems claustrophobic and offers very little escape from the outside world. Stanley beats Stella, Eunice and Steve fight constantly. They are like sardines in a very small can. More importantly Blanche is increasingly trapped, especially as Stanley discovers the truth about her.

Scene 10 is where New Orleans seems at its most violent. Stanley is threatening Blanche and she has nowhere to go. The back wall of the apartment fades and reveals a clear scrim and the audience looks through to the street outside. A prostitute is stealing from a drunk and a policeman blows his whistle. This is the darker side to the French Quarter. What is happening outside reflects on what is happening inside because just after this tableau Stanley attacks Blanche. Williams is expressing the darker side to what appears on the surface to be an exciting, contented place.

SOME USEFUL SETTING QUOTES

'This section is poor, but unlike corresponding sections in other American cities, it has a raffish charm.'

'This Blue Piano' expresses the sprit of life which goes on here.'

'Only Poe! Only Mr Edgar Allan Poe! -Could do it justice!'
(BLANCHE)

'It's not that bad at all. New Orleans isn't like other cities.'
(STELLA)

'I guess we strike you as being a pretty rough bunch'
(MITCH)

SETTING QUESTIONS

❑ Elysian Fields is compared to Stella and Blanche's family home, Belle Reve. How are the two contrasted?

❑ Sound is vital to establishing the setting. List some of the different sounds of the city that occur during important moments in the play.

❑ When Blanche mentions she has nice clothes to meet Stella's friends in Stella replies 'I'm afraid they won't think they are lovely.' Why wouldn't they?

❑ What does the interior setting of Stanley and Stella's apartment suggest about the lifestyle of this area?

❑ Stanley and Mitch work for a car manufacturing plant. Is this important to the setting? Why?

❑ The name 'Elysian Fields' is an apt title for Stanley and Stella's street. Why?

❑In Scene 10 the back walls become transparent. What does the audience see and what does it represent?

❑ Why does Williams choose to have the play set in such a multi-cultural type area?

CHARACTER ANALYSIS

BLANCHE DuBOIS

Blanche is an English teacher with a lot of secrets to hide. When she first appears on stage the audience is aware of none of them, only that this is a very gentile, highly-strung woman who doesn't seem to fit into the French Quarter. As the play unfolds and her past and tenuous future become apparent it is admirable that she tries so hard to maintain her dignity.

Her appearance is described as 'moth-like'. Paradoxically, she has a strong aversion to light. She tells Mitch that she, 'can't stand a naked light bulb any more than I can a rude remark or vulgar action.' This is a fascinating aspect of her character, because at first it may seem that she uses the dark to deceive people like Mitch about her age and past. On another level it suggests her utter devastation at everything she has had to go through. When she describes the suicide of her husband she says, 'the searchlight which had been turned on the world was turned off again and never for one moment has there been any light that's brighter than this-kitchen candle...'

At first Blanche may not appear all that likeable. Her comments to Stella about 'this horrible place!' seem unfair and snobbish. She has many pretensions, at the poker night she grandly declares to the players, 'please don't get up'. She has an awful vanity; constantly needing assurance about her looks and avoiding any light so no one can have a good a look at her and how old she is. At this level she represents a dieing breed-the southern belle.

Her position as part of the elite plantation farmers who held such a high position in the past puts her in direct conflict with her brother-in-law Stanley, a modern working-class man, for the affection and attention of Stella. She tries to make Stella feel guilty about leaving Belle Reve to marry Stanley, saying that she was left alone with the burden of keeping the family together. She attempts to get her to leave Stanley after he hits her, pleading, 'don't hang back with the brutes!' But Stella faces the harsh realties of the modern world and chooses Stanley.

It is open to interpretation how much of Blanche's behaviour is manipulation and how much of it is proof of her gradual mental deterioration. Clearly her heavy drinking, constant nervous jumps at noises suggest someone who is not well. The lies about he old beau Shep Huntley coming to rescue her, her age and vagueness about why she isn't working appear calculated. The catch is does Blanche actually believe in the world she has created? Clearly by the end of the play when Stanley confronts her with the truth and Mitch refuses to marry her she is lost. She puts on her ball gown and tries to charm imaginary suitors. When confronted with the truth she cannot survive, she needs 'the magic' of love and desire to block out what she has faced.

So what exactly is real about Blanche? She arrives in Elysian Fields because after Belle Reve was lost she was forced to rely on 'intimacies with many strangers' to survive. An affair with a 17-year-old student was the last straw and she was forced out of her hometown, Laurel. Her need for survival was not just physical but emotional because of the death of all of her family except Stella and the suicide of her young husband Alan Grey. She was responsible for it because she told him discovering his homosexuality disgusted her. Her immoral behaviour was simply an attempt to gain protection and find joy in life again. But her deceptions have no place in the harsh world of Elysian Fields and Stanley's brutal attack at the end of scene 10 is too much for her. She cannot belong here; a doctor packs her off to a mental institution. In her eyes she is finally saved by the kindness of a stranger. The audience cannot help but feel pity for by the end of the play

Some Useful 'Blanche' Quotes

'But you are the one that abandoned Belle Reve, not I! I stayed and fought for it, bled for it, almost died for it!'

'Soft people have got to court the favour of hard ones, Stella...make a little-temporary magic just in order to pay —one night's shelter!'

'I want to *rest*! I want to breathe quietly again! Yes-I want Mitch... *very badly*!'

'The searchlight which had been turned on the world was turned off again and never for one moment has there been any light that's greater than this-kitchen candle...'

'Whoever you are-I have always depended on the kindness of strangers.'

STANLEY KOWALSKI

The audience feels as if they understand Stanley the first time he appears on stage chatting with his buddies and throwing Stella a lump of meat. He is straightforward and uncomplicated. Yet there is darker side to him that is uncovered throughout the play. Like Blanche, there are many contradictions within him. How can someone so volatile and down-to-earth as Stanley have married Stella and impress his boss enough to be a travelling sales representative?

There are some pretty obvious facts about Stanley. He is a blue-collar worker of Polish descent. He likes bowling and playing poker with his buddies. He has a strong violent streak. He, shouts, hurls radios out windows, overturns furniture, beats his wife at least once and rapes Blanche. He has a great appetite for sex. Williams tells us that, '*He sizes women up at a glance, with sexual classifications, crude images flashing into his mind and determining the way he looks at them.*'

However there is a softer and compassionate side to him. His deep love for Stella is clearly depicted at the end of scene three when he screams, 'STELLAHHHHHH!' over and over again to get her to return. When she does return and they tenderly embrace he mumbles, 'don't ever leave me...don't ever leave me...sweetheart...baby...' He has a great sense of humour too. When Blanche is trying up the bathroom and she asks him to 'posses you soul in patience!' he responds with 'It's not my soul I'm worried about!'

At the beginning the audience feels sorry for him. He has to share his cramped apartment with a snobbish middle-aged sister-in-law who clearly wants to remove Stella from this environment.

Stanley's motivation for his destruction of Blanche has been debated extensively. Clearly they are adversaries right from the start. They have completely different backgrounds. Stanley points out that Blanche's hometown Laurel is 'not my territory'. What's more they both want the complete attention and affection of Stella.

Stanley's investigations into Blanche's recent history begin because he is worried he and Stella have been swindled out of some money from the sale of Belle Reve, and as he says, 'I don't like to be swindled. 'He cannot stand to be fooled. When he finds out the truth he is motivated by clear intentions to bring everything out into the open. This is understandable especially as his war-buddy Mitch is involved with Blanche and he doesn't want to see him hurt, he tries to explain to Stella that, 'I'd have that on my conscience the rest of my life if I knew all that stuff and let my best friend get caught!'

It is also understandable that he is worried about his relationship with Stella. When Blanche arrives their lives are turned upside down. She is very demanding-getting Stella to make her drinks all the time and constantly needing to be told she is beautiful. He is worried for Stella and their baby.

There is pride involved too. Blanche makes it very clear she doesn't think Stella should stay in this place. She represents an easier, more relaxed time in Stella's life when she had far more luxurious conditions. This starts to affect Stella. At Blanche's birthday dinner she tells him that, 'your face and your fingers are disgustingly greasy. Go wash up and then help me clear the table.' He cannot stand his superiority being questioned. He grabs the plates off the table and smashes them. The excuse of his buddy Mitch and his howling for Stella seem hollow now. Raping Blanche finally means he has victory over her; he has power back because Stella won't believe Blanche. She can't because Stanley is her best chance of a future for her and their baby. However it is still contentious whether Stanley fully wins at the end or has Stella, and their life together, been changed?

Some Useful 'Stanley' Quotes

'He sizes women up at a glance, with sexual classifications, crude images flashing into his mind and determining the way he looks at them.'

'Don't ever leave me...don't ever leave me...sweetheart...baby...'

'It's not my soul I'm worried about!'

'I pulled you down off them columns and how you loved it, having them coloured lights going!'

I'd have that on my conscience the rest of my life if I knew all that stuff and let my best friend get caught!'

'I've been on to you from the start! Not once did you pull any wool over this boy's eyes!'

STELLA KOWALSKI

Stella is a simple and sweet woman. Her story is fairly uncomplicated. She moved to New Orleans to work and make her own life, met Stanley and married him. At the beginning of the play she is pregnant with their first child. She has broken from her past and embraced her life in the French Quarter.

Stanley and Stella are such opposites in many ways it is surprising she chose to marry him. She is gentle and he is violent. Stanley is active and Stella is passive. He makes heaps of noise as he yells and bangs things when he's angry while she has a quiet nature. When he is rummaging through Blanche's trunk at the beginning her only response is, 'Shhh! Be still Stanley!'

It becomes clear that what sustains this marriage is not compatibility but their love and all consuming passion for each other. Stella talks about being thrilled at Stanley's temper when he smashed all the light bulbs on their wedding night. Stanley delights in the fact he dragged her down from the white columns of Belle Reve and into bed. Stella clearly adores him and the little home they've created sighing, 'I can hardly stand it when he's away for a night...'

Her relationship with Blanche is a testy one. She wants desperately to please her, like any little sister does. She didn't tell Blanche exactly how different her apartment was from Belle Reve. She waits on her hand and foot. She sits obediently while Blanche criticises her home as 'dreadful conditions' and Stanley as 'common'. Her reply is simply, 'Why, yes, I suppose he is'. There is an unconscious hostility apparent in Stella that manifests itself several times. When Blanche tries to convince her to leave Stanley she is adamant that, 'I'm not in anything I want to get out of.'

There has been much analysis of Stella's position at the end of the play. She has chosen to send Blanche off to a mental institution rather than believe her. Is this an acceptance of the reality that to survive she needs Stanley? Or does it suggest she has created her own illusions instead of believing Blanche's story? Has Blanche's invasion of their world had any impact on her? Stella's complete devastation at the end of the play would suggests perhaps her little paradise won't be quite the same.

Some Useful 'Stella' quotes

'I can hardly stand it when he's away for a night...'

'Your face and your fingers are disgustingly greasy. Go wash up and then help me clear the table.'

'Blanche, I'd forgotten how excitable you are. You're making too much fuss about this.'

'But there's things that happen between a man and a woman in the dark-that sort of make everything else-seem-unimportant'

'But people like you abused her, and forced her to change.'

'I don't know if I did the right thing.'

HAROLD MITCHELL (MITCH)

Mitch, as he prefers to be called is a sweet gentle bachelor. He is a little dull and self-conscious. He still lives with his frail, elderly mother.

While he does not seem to be classically good looking or intelligent he is honest and caring. He does not fit in well with Stanley's poker crowd. They are always teasing him. As Blanche points out when she first meets him, 'that one seems-superior to the others.' However, he is not anything like the rich young gentlemen who used to command her attention. Perhaps this is why Blanche chooses him. She sees how Stella has made a life for herself with Stanley and feels she could do the same with Mitch.

Mitch seems very insecure. He constantly makes references to his height and weight. He also frets about his mother. In almost every single scene he is in he mentions her. He feels incredible guilt when he is not at home and looking after her. He also is worried about when she dies, and the fact he will be alone after that. He begins to see Blanche as a possibility for a happy life. This is especially the case at the end of scene 6 when he comments, 'you need somebody and I need somebody, too. Could it be-you and me, Blanche?'

Blanche comes to depend on Mitch as her last chance for survival. She tells Stella, 'I want to *rest!* I want to breathe quietly again!' Blanche believes that if she marries Mitch this will happen. She'll have someone to depend on and won't have to keep living with Stella and Stanley.

At first glance Mitch and Blanche seem incompatible. The audience sees that earlier on in scene 5, when Blanche and Mitch's date begins so awkwardly. Mitch is not a southern gentleman, but a modern man with needs. Demure Blanche cannot cope with this. Stella adapted to Stanley, but Blanche still lives in her make-believe world of charm and manners. She prefers to pretend that she is chaste because she wants his respect. Mitch responds well to this-not even kissing her without asking first. There is a genuine connection between the two and their determination not to be lonely would have made their marriage work. They have both lost lovers-Mitch's sad story about the inscription on his cigarette holder immediately gives them a bond. This makes Stanley's possibly well-intentioned intrusion particularly unwelcome.

When Mitch finds out the truth about Blanche from Stanley it is a shock. Reality is a problem with Mitch. Mitch does not cope with Blanche's lies. When he finds out he feels his manhood is on the line, he has been fooled. He tries to force himself on Blanche to vent his anger but is too distraught to do it. He simply retreats defeated.

In the final scene there is clear tension between Stanley and Mitch. Mitch probably knows Stanley raped Blanche and is distressed at seeing her with no grip on reality. He also regrets Stanley's intrusions and the two men actually come to blows. Mitch wishes he had been kept in the dark, saying, 'You! You done this with all a your God-damn rutting with things you...' Clearly Mitch wishes he had stayed in Blanche's illusionary world.

EUNICE AND STEVE HUBBELL

Eunice and Steve own the apartment building where Stanley and Stella rent the first floor apartment. They are close friends and Eunice in particular is protective of Stella like an aunt or big sister. This is specially seen when she gives Stella refuge from Stanley after he hit her and tells him to stay away from her.

Steve is one of Stanley's drinking, poker and bowling buddies. He is typically one of the boys hanging around at the poker nights. Crass and slovenly-he gives a good picture of what the lifestyle is like in the French Quarter.

Steve and Eunice represent what life will be like for Stanley and Stella in 20 or so years. Fighting and lovemaking is a regular cycle in their lives. At first glance they may seem unhappy but they are deeply in love. After one fight where Eunice threatens to call the police the next time they appear, '*Steve's arm is around Eunice's shoulder and she is sobbing luxuriously and he is cooing love words.*'

Eunice accepts her philandering and sometimes-violent husband because she cannot survive otherwise. She is a realist who knows how the world works. It is Eunice that tells Stella not to believe Blanche's story about the rape, 'don't ever believe it. Life has got to go on. No matter what happens, you've got to keep on going.'

PABLO GONZALES

Pablo is another poker, beer and bowling buddy. Like Steve he is crass and slovenly. His Spanish contributes to the sense of New Orleans being a vibrant melting pot.

THE YOUNG COLLECTOR

He represents the innocence-the child in Blanche's English class, her husband Allan and her own gentle youth that has been lost. Their conversation is child-like talk of cherry soda and rain. She kisses him to feel that innocence again

THE STRANGE MAN AND WOMAN

They are known to Blanche as the strange man and woman because when they appear at the end of the play she is has no grip on reality. They are a doctor and nurse sent to accompany Blanche to the asylum. While the nurse tries to force Blanche into a straight jacket and cut her nails the doctor knows a softer approach is needed. Her gives her dignity by taking her hand and treating her like a beau would.

FRENCH QUARTER RESIDENTS

Other characters such as the "Negro Woman", the Mexican flower seller and the street vendor represent the inhabitants of New Orleans-many and varied. Their sounds increasingly invade Blanche's head. The Mexican woman also gives an insight into the dark corners of Blanche's mind when she repeatedly calls out '*Flores. Flores para los muertos.*' (Flowers for the dead).

CHARACTER QUESTIONS

❑ Does Blanche really believe in the fantasy world she has created? Find evidence-for or against.

❑ Trace Blanche's decline into insanity. Is she unstable right from the start?

❑ What aspects of Stanley's character make him sympathetic for the audience?

❑ Describe some of the contrasts that are made between Stanley and Blanche.

❑ Do you think Stella has really decided not to believe Blanche?

❑ Mitch seems to genuinely care about Blanche. Why does he believe Stanley so easily then?

❑ Why does Eunice tell Stella she shouldn't believe Blanche?

❑ Make a list of minor characters. How do they contribute to the atmosphere of New Orleans?

❑ Who is Shep Huntley and what purpose does he serve?

THEMATIC CONCERNS

THE VICTORY OF THE APES

Throughout the play characters are described as animals. Sounds and behaviours are described as animalistic. Stanley is depicted as apelike and as a, ' a richly feathered male bird'. Mitch dances like a bear. Women chatter like hens. The atmosphere of a humid climate punctuated by shrieks and moans in the distance makes the French Quarter seem jungle-like.

Blanche is a definite contrast to this jungle world. She is civilisation. She believes in the importance of romance and poetry. She has old-fashioned ideals about behaviour and dress. In scene three she wonders whether it is appropriate for her to be on the steps outside the house with only a dressing gown on. Mitch replies, 'that makes no difference in the quarter'. She can't believe Stella has found herself in such a place with very common people. She gives a grand speech about Stanley depicting all his 'ape-like' qualities and lamenting the loss of civilisation. Blanche begs with her 'don't hang back with the brutes!' It almost sways Stella but not quite. Stella has moved on but Blanche clings to the memories of their home Belle Reve, as the way life should be lived.

So if Blanche is the champion of civilisation does that make Stanley a brute or merely a modern man adept at surviving in a harsh world? Clearly Stanley lives in the present. This is not necessarily negative He questions Blanche about the loss of Belle Reve because he is concerned with money and acquiring whatever is rightfully his.

Blanche's family lost the property through mismanagement and centuries of 'epic fornications'. It is not right or wrong that Stanley and his fellow apes win their battle-both for the world and simply the affection of Stella. It is the grim truth that they have what it takes to survive-a grip on reality. However Williams is also saying that it is regrettable that it comes at the expense of Blanche. She finishes the play utterly hopeless and forced into a mental institution because of Stanley's attack. The audience laments her destruction.

REALITY VERSUS ILLUSION or REALISM VERSUS IDEALISM

Stanley and Stanley inhabit the very real world of New Orleans. Blanche creates a make-believe world full of lies and illusions. These two worlds consistently clash throughout the play.

Blanche refers many times to what she believes ought to be true. She defends her lies by calling it magic that is needed to survive. Blanche tells Mitch, 'I don't want realism'. It is easy to see why. Reality, for her, forced her husband to commit suicide. It meant losing her family and home. Leaving her destitute, lonely and old. She tells so many lies both little ones about her age to big ones about the reason for visiting Stella and Stanley. These are the lies needed for her to survive, by staying with Stella and Stanley and perhaps eventually marrying Mitch.

The lies eventually take over as she starts to dwell in these illusions. She cannot accept what her life has become and instead retreats to a time that was carefree and wonderful. She was gorgeous and surrounded by admirers. She believes that this is the world that should exist-one of love and kindness. She covers up light bulbs to deflect the outside world and prevent it from seeing what she has become.

Blanche's illusions are a coping mechanism for all the loss she has suffered. Sometimes dreams seem much better than real life...

While Blanche covers light bulbs Stanley, quite literally, smashes them. He cannot allow even half-truths he needs everything open and straightforward. He has to know all the details about the loss of Belle Reve, and why Blanche is visiting them. He speaks his mind. When Blanche asks him how she looks he says 'your looks are okay' and explains he doesn't compliment women because it's unnecessary. He believes if they are good looking they know it. He tells Mitch and Stella about Blanche's past because he cannot stand keeping it from them. Also he cannot stand to be fooled. He gloats in scene 10 that Blanche never pulled wool over his eyes.

The dilemma the audience is faced with is which is better: reality or illusion. Williams shows that both worlds are cruel. The conclusion that can be reached is that ultimately idealists like Blanche don't have much of a place in modern society.

LONELINESS

A Streetcar Named Desire is filled with lonely people. They all want an end to the pain and emptiness of being alone.

Blanche comes to Elysian Fields completely isolated. She is living with the death of her young husband Alan Grey, losing her family, home and the life that she knew. Her brief sexual encounters were an attempt to find comfort and respite from the reality she is now by herself but have now become a source of shame as she is forced out of Laurel. She comes to Stella, hoping to be welcomed with open arms and instead becomes an intruder. It is the same reason she invents a long lost relationship with Shep Huntley. She needs to feel loved. Her many lies about her age and past are all in an effort to stay with Stella. She is her only chance. When she realises that perhaps Stella won't leave Stanley, she latches on to Mitch in complete desperation, hoping a marriage will fix all her problems. As she tells Stella, 'I *can't* be *alo*ne!'

Mitch is also lonely. He has an affinity with Blanche that is established early on when he show his cigarette holder engraved with a message from a dead lover. He is left to look after his dieing mother and she is all he has. As he explains to his poker buddies, 'you all are married. But I'll be alone when she goes.' He views his relationship with Blanche as an attempt to find a replacement for his mother.

Other characters are lonely too. Eunice resents Steve being out all the time. Stanley goes ballistic at the possibility of losing Stella. Stella cannot cope when Stanley is away. She confesses to Blanche that, 'When he's away for a week I nearly go wild!' Clearly it is not only Blanche who lacks love and companionship.

Tennessee Williams is expressing, through these characters, the fear we all have of spending our lives alone.

DESIRE

Desire is a constantly present throughout the play. It is made obvious y the very sexual overtones of the play. This is present in the story of Alan Grey, Blanche's unsavoury relations with students and ultimately the rape of Blanche. Stella and Stanley are passionate and almost violent in their lovemaking (we get suggestions of this in scene four, the morning after the poker night).

While Blanche is critical of this calling 'common' and 'brutal 'the audience becomes well aware of her own transgressions. The audience becomes uncomfortable with Blanche's current behaviour when they realise her past. Stanley and Stella seem natural and healthy in comparison. However it would go to far to say, 'she asked for it', which is what Stanley clearly believes.

Blanche does not believe in desire purely for it's own sake. She explains that, 'the opposite of death is desire'. It is an affirmation that she has survived and that she is still alive. Stella and Stanley whose need for each other is completely physical and almost animalistic only confirm this. They feel no shame in their actions, a complete contrast to Blanche's veneer of prudishness.

OLD AND NEW AMERICA

Just as Blanche is illusion and Stanley reality Blanche is America's past and Stanley is it's future (as it looked in 1940's when William wrote the play)

Blanche is part of a rapidly declining world. She represents the 'old south' where rich white families ruled like aristocrats over their plantations. Their wealth was entirely agriculturally based. Her struggles to survive mirror that of this society in general.

Stanley is the perfect picture of where America was heading in the 1940s. Having won the war and armed with new technology and wealth Americans were desperate for a new start. Stanley is part of this modern commercialism- working for a manufacturing plant. Wealth was to be earned not inherited. A person of Polish decent, he also represents the immigrants who made America such a melting pot. This new world had no place for some one like Blanche.

THEME QUESTIONS

❏ Find as many animal references throughout the play as you can. What kind of animal is Blanche?

❏ Does Stella belong in the real or illusionary world?

❏ Who do Blanche's illusions actually damage?

❏ Mitch sees Blanche as a potential replacement for his mother. What role does Mitch have for Blanche?

❏ Stanley and Stella aren't the only ones consumed by desire. Find some other examples in minor characters throughout the play. How do they reflect on Blanche?

❏ What does the story of Blanche's family suggest about the real cause of Blanche's situation?

THEATRICAL TECHNIQUES AND LANGUAGE

A Streetcar Named Desire is essentially an expressionistic play that examines real characters, a real place and real moral dilemmas. Laden with symbols and theatrics, it is sometimes easy to forget that at the heart of this play are fragile people dealing with complex situations.

Williams makes many scenes like pieces of art. In fact there is an introduction to scene 3 (The Poker Night) that suggests the scene is reminiscent of a Van Gogh painting of a billiard parlour at night.

Williams believed expressionism should not diminish the real aspects in a play. He argued that,

'When a play employs unconventional

techniques it is not, or certainly shouldn't

be, trying to escape its responsibilities of

dealing with reality, or interpreting

experience, but is actually or should be

attempting to find a closer approach, a more

penetrating and vivid expression of things as

they are.'

STAGE

The setting is made very obvious on stage. We are told that on stage is a tall old building with two levels. Most of the action takes place in the lower level-Stanley and Stella's apartment. Lighting illuminates the parts that are being used.

The apartment itself is supposed to be cluttered. It changes gradually during the play as characters make and clean up various messes.

PROPS

There are many props that form part of the everyday actions of the characters. Important ones seem to be Blanche's suitcase and it's contents, alcohol bottles, clothes and food.

Most remain on stage throughout the play even after they've been used and suggest the passing of time. Stanley, for example, often changes his clothes and leaves shirts lying around the stage. Williams wanted his characters to be as realistic as possible and having them interact with props makes them identifiable. For instance Blanche's shaking as she lights her cigarette or pours a drink emphasis her nervousness.

STAGE DIRECTIONS

Williams's stage directions are long and detailed. He describes characters movements, and also how should feel as they make these movements. When Blanche first enters the apartment Wilder writes, *'Blanche sits in a chair very stiffly with her shoulders slightly hunched and her legs pressed close together and her hands tightly clutching her purse as if she were quite cold.'* The audience is automatically aware how uncomfortable and how nervous she is already.

The stage directions are also incredibly poetic. Williams gives grand descriptions of how a scene should look and feel. In scene 10 as Stanley is threatening Blanche Williams tells us that, '*the night is filed with inhuman voices like cries in the jungle. The shadows and lurid reflections move sinuously as flame along the wall spaces.*'

BLOCKING

Blocking is usually a technique employed by directors of specific productions and not specified by the playwright. The positioning of characters on the stage in this play should be realistic. It is designed to show them interacting with each other. There are some important elements that must be considered when blocking-for example the increasing threat Stanley poses to Blanche and how scared she becomes of him, or the passion of Stanley and Stella's relationship

SOUND EFFECTS/MUSIC

Sound effects and music are a constant throughout the play.

The "Blue Piano" is vital to establishing the mood and the setting. It is suggestive a vibrant culture surrounding the apartment.

The Varsouviana is a classical piece that is only ever heard in Blanche's head. It is the music that was playing when Blanche told her husband she knew his horrible secret and moments later he shot himself-that is why it is always finished with a gunshot. It represents her guilt and trauma over his death.

Many noises are heard throughout the play. The sounds of the nearby trains, thunder, cats screeching, yells from the street create the atmosphere of New Orleans. They are also the exterior world invading Blanche's interior thoughts. Increasingly the audience becomes confused as to whether the noises are real or just in Blanche's head

Another nice musical touch is Blanche's 'paper moon' song. Blanche's bright, happy singing is juxtaposed with Stanley and Stella's bitter quarrel as he tells her the truth about Blanche.' Blanche, yet again is in her own world of love songs and Stanley is dealing with cold hard facts and reality.

LIGHTING

Williams uses the concept of light and dark, shadow and illumination to represent reality. Blanche lives in a world of darkness-covering light bulbs and only being viewed in the shadows. In contrast Stanley searches for the light-and even smashes light bulbs.

Lighting also expresses he mood of various scenes. In scene three, 'The Poker Night' Williams says, '*the kitchen now suggests that sort of lurid nocturnal brilliance, the raw colours of childhood's spectrum, Over the yellow linoleum hangs an electric bulb with a vivid green glass shade.*' This is a scene dominated by the men of the French Quarter. They are crude, energetic and earthy. The raw bright light from an electric light bulb sets the scene for them.

On another level the lighting in the play is merely functional. Different rooms or sections of the stage are illuminated as characters are using them. Ones not being used are in darkness. This allows the audience to focus on what is happening.

COSTUMING

There are very specific clothes that Williams suggest characters should wear to emphasise their qualities.

Blanche wears faux sophisticated clothing-silk robes and white skirts. She gives an air of glamour and tells Stanley that, 'Clothes are my passion'. The audience gradually becomes aware that the clothes she wears are old-relics of the past she is desperate to cling onto.

Stanley constantly changes clothes and exposes his chest-highlighting his masculinity. His clothes suggest a working class man who doesn't particularly care much about his appearance.

Stella wears pale, simple dresses. As a housewife in 'The Quarter' she doesn't have to dress up for anything. She fades into the background next to Blanche, as she probably did when they were young.

CONFLICTS

The conflicts present in *A Streetcar Named Desire* are many. They exist between characters and between individual characters and larger elements.

STANLEY AND BLANCHE

This is perhaps the most obvious conflict. They are opposites in every possible way. The controversial element is the huge amount of sexual tension evident in all their exchanges. Blanche openly flirts with Stanley and he looks her up and down constantly. It would be going to far to say it excuses Stanley's attack but it makes theirs an unsettling conflict that exists on every possible level.

Stanley cannot stand Blanche's intrusion into what he sees as Stella and his otherwise happy existence. She threatens his supremacy. He is well aware that she finds him, 'common', because he overhears her pleading with Stella to leave him in scene 4. She is the only character who really questions his supremacy and he cannot stand it.

Their conflict is centred on Stella but at a wider level it is also a battle for control of society (as they represent old and new America).

STELLA AND BLANCHE

This is a more subtle conflict but one that is in the background of their relationship. Stella grows weary of Blanche's demanding nature and insecurities. Her comments on how beautiful she seem strained. Perhaps in their previous life at Belle Rev Stella was a little jealous of Blanche and her many admirers. Or perhaps Blanche was always dismissive of her. Stella mentions how she used to wait on Blanche all the time at home. She also refers to Blanche's 'flighty' behaviour even before she left Belle Reve. She obviously disapproves of her sister. At the same time she is desperate to please her, lying about life in

Elysian Fields in letters so Blanche wouldn't look down on here.

STELLA AND STANLEY

At first they may seem the perfect couple. They are genuinely in love and have a passionate relationship. There are obvious tensions though, and they are exacerbated when Blanche arrives. When Stanley hits her we are not sure whether it is the first time he has. Stella's behaviour after and Mitch's comments that it's a shame it happened while Blanche was here suggests perhaps not. Blanche reminds Stella of the grand life she used to have and Stanley can't stand that. Stella gets increasingly angry at Stanley's treatment of Blanche that reaches boiling point when he gives her a one-way ticket home. She tells him that, 'people like you abused her and forced her to change'. The end of the play is ambiguous. Does Stella really think Blanche lied about the rape or has she suddenly seen her husband for what he is?

BLANCHE AND REALITY/NEW ORLEANS

Blanche is completely contradictory to everything that exists in Elysian Fields. This is immediately established when she first appears dressed immaculately in white and wearing gloves. Eunice tries to be friendly by showing her Stanley and Stella's apartment but is met with Blanche asking to be left alone. She cannot adapt to life there at all.

Blanche's battle for sanity becomes more and more desperate as the play progresses. While at the beginning her lies can be viewed as pure manipulation towards the end she appears to genuinely believe in her fantasy world. She tries hard to find an escape-through Stella and Mitch but Stanley's cruel behaviour puts an end to that. Blanche loses her battle and retreats into her delusions.

LANGUAGE

As has already been mentioned, Williams is an extremely poetic playwright. Such poetry is beautifully fitting for Blanche, an English schoolteacher with a love of refined culture. She compares Elysian Fields to the work of the great Edgar Alan Poe, 'out there I suppose is the ghoul-haunted woodland of Weir!' She makes many melodramatic statements like this. It serves to further alienate her from the other characters and emphasise her refined nature.

The inhabitants of the French Quarter speak realistically. There is no pretension in their speech, just straight talking. When Blanche makes her Poe comment Stella replies, 'no honey those are the L&N tracks.'

As well as the plain dialogue there are many colloquialisms that creep into the play.' Stanley, in particular has some earthy expressions such as, 'You're damn tootin'. The Negro woman, designed to add authentic atmosphere speaks in a similarly relaxed fashion, greeting the young collector with, 'hey sugar!' Their language makes the audience realise these people inhabit a very particular time and place-New Orleans in the 1940s.

SYMBOLS

SHEP HUNTLEY

Apparently an old college beau of Blanche's, Shep is a symbol of the perfect gentlemen for whom Blanche searched but never found. She creates him as her knight in shining armour. Blanche rings him in scene 10 because she feels threatened by Stanley. In scene 4, after Stanley hit Stella she also tries to contact him, 'darling Shep. Sister and I in desperate situation.' By the final scene she really believes he will rescue her and take her on a cruise in the Caribbean. The image Blanche paints of him; wealthy, dashing, sensitive and respectful indicate some one obviously not real but who should be, at least for Blanche's sake. He seems to contrast with Mitch, who is awkward and fumbling as he gives Blanche flowers and takes pride in his height and weight.

VASUVIANA

The Varsouviana is significant as an expression of the guilt in Blanche's mind over the death of Alan Grey. Each time she hears the music she recalls the night he killed himself, ending with a gunshot. The music becomes louder and is repeated increasingly as the play goes on. This suggests Blanche's deterioration

'PAPER MOON' SONG

'*Say it's only a paper moon. Sailing over cardboard sea -But it wouldn't be make –believe if you believed in me!'*

'It's a Barnum and Bailey world. Just as phoney as can be!'

*'Without your love
It's a honky-tonk parade
Without your love
It's a melody played in a penny arcade...'*

Blanche sings this song in scene seven, just as Stanley is telling Stella the sordid truth about Blanche's recent behaviour. It is a song about the magic of make-believe and love. This is the world Blanche is in and the one she needs other people to believe in to. It suggests that lies aren't that bad if they come from love and help make the world more bearable. That is Blanche's entire philosophy.

It juxtaposed quite cleverly with Stanley and Stella's row. Just as Blanche is singing about lies and make-believe Stanley is forcing his wife to understand the truth about Blanche. He gives all the explicit details of affairs with strangers, soldiers and even students. This 'paper moon' blanche so cherishes is being torn apart.

'FLOWERS FOR THE DEAD'.

In the play we are never sure if the Mexican woman is really there or a figment of Blanche's mind. She adds to the mood of the French Quarter. She appears selling flowers at a time when Blanche is most desperate because Mitch is abandoning her. Her calling out 'flowers for the dead' is symbolic of Blanche's destiny or fate. The only escape for Blanche from the harsh reality of commercialised life in post war America is now death. Her failure to cope with reality means she has failed to remain among the living.

ELYSIAN FIELDS

It is no accident that this is the address for Stanley and Stella. Elysian Fields, in Greek Mythology means paradise. It is where all great heroes spend their afterlife. In the play it is where Stanley and Stella live. It is symbolic of the sensual and blissful 'paradise' they have created. The references he makes to coloured lights swirling shows that Stanley at least sees their home as magical. But it has the opposite effect on Blanche as she encounters only sorrow and destruction there. Elysian Fields, just the same as that other paradise-The Garden of Eden, was only created for two. Blanche is merely an intruder here.

DESIRE AND CEMETRIES

Desire and Cemeteries are used to name the streetcars Blanche travels on (apparently the names of real streetcars Williams saw running outside his New Orleans home). They are extremely appropriate transportation for Blanche. Desire symbolises Blanche's need for love and understanding but always in the background lurks the fear of death and destruction. If desire can't be obtained a 'transfer to cemeteries' will be inevitable. Desire therefore becomes the opposite of death.

COLOURS

Blanche talks a lot about colour-she distinguishes between pale and dark commenting that Stanley must like 'strong primary colours'. His shirts are described as vibrant and colourful. This is another way of expressing passion for life. Blanche desperately wants life. She says she dislikes pale colours, yet that seems to be all she wears. She has been so hurt by life she now can only stand a pale imitation of it

FOOD AND DRINK

Food and drink are vital elements to the play. Drink has many connotations. Blanche's constant drinking is a clear indication of her mental imbalances. When she some drink is spilt on her skirt she becomes nearly hysterical, showing she is fast deterioration. Blanche and Mitch share a drink of aptly named, 'Southern Comfort'. In scene 10 Stanley opens a bottle between his knees in a movement full of phallic suggestiveness, before asking her if she wants to make it, 'a loving cup.'

The sharing of a meal is an indication of who is winning the battle. In scene 3 Stella and Blanche go to Galatiore's for dinner while Stanley is left with only cold cuts. During Blanche's ruined birthday party Stanley eats like a king, stuffing himself with chops. Meanwhile Stella hardly touches her food. When Blanche receives her ticket back to Laurel she races to the bathroom and gagging sounds are heard. Clearly it is only the victorious who feast.

EXPRESSIONISM/ SYMBOLISM

A Streetcar Named Desire is full of expressionistic techniques. It is a play that pulls out every theatrical element and uses them to express Williams's many concerns.

THE OUTWARD EXPRESSION OF BLANCHE'S INNER THOUGHTS

Williams did not simply want the audience to understand Blanche purely through her actions (which most of the time are so contradictory). He chose to display her inner torments on stage.

The sounds of the city and the sounds of the past increasingly invade Blanche. Every sudden noise such as cats screeching or trains rattling past disturbs her. Finally in scene 11 strange voices call her. The audience does not just see her reaction to them but actually hears the on stage.

The repetition of the Varsouviana expresses Blanche's guilt over the death of her young husband. It ends with the shot that killed him.

STRUCTURE

There are eleven scenes occurring chronologically between May and September. There are typically two intermissions. This divides the play into three sections that help to express the battle between Blanche and Stanley. The first act ends at scene 4 when Stella tells Blanche she will not be leaving Stanley. This is a loss for Blanche. The second act ends at scene 6, after Mitch and Blanche's date, where she has clearly won his affections. It is a victory for her. The play concludes with Blanche leaves for the mental institution following Stanley's rape. That is his ultimate victory and her tragic loss.

The structure revolves around the spoiled occasion. This expresses the loneliness and solitude the characters (and indeed all people) sometimes feel. The first act centres on a poker night that breaks up when Stanley hits Stella. The second act mentions how Blanche and Mitch's date is awkward because of their differences and her nervousness. The third act deals with Blanche's birthday. Scene 7 is the ruined party, Mitch not appearing because he has been told everything by Stanley. An empty chair sits there eloquently expressing Blanche's loss. The cake is never eaten or the candles lit. The play ends with a second poker game. This game does not fully stop this time despite Blanche's departure-not for a cruise ship but an asylum.

LIGHTING

The lighting of the play expresses the concept of reality versus illusion. Blanche constantly covers light bulbs with lanterns or turns them off. She cannot face reality. Stanley, we are told, smashed light bulbs on his wedding night. He inhabits the real world and is determined to discover the truth about Blanche.

REALISM

What is most striking about this play is the rawness and truth of the characters and the setting. Williams used his own experiences-of growing up in the south and living in New Orleans to bring it alive on stage.

CHARACTERS

All the characters in this play face real life struggles, conflicts and emotions. They speak, as you'd expect these kinds of people to-whether the loud New Orleans exclamations or Blanche's mannered southern drawl. These characters are not overly melodramatic (accept Blanche but that is explained) considering what they go through. We see how desperate they all are for kindness and connection with each other. We feel for them. We are also given the reasons why they are so lonely or desperate. Stella is left in this tiny apartment alone for long stretches. Stanley can't shake the feeling Stella may question his superiority. Blanche has faced death, guilt, rejection and humiliation.

Stanley is perhaps the most 'real' of all the characters. His loudness and violence explode in front of the audience and we are left in little doubt as to what kind of person he is. He has an authentic working class type of speech-punctuated with lots of 'damn!' and 'yeah'. The first and probably the most infamous) portrayal of him was by Marlon Brando. Brando was a close follower of Stanislavsky's Method acting style, which focussed on actor's using his or her own memories to help understand a character. The aim was not merely to represent a character but to get as close as possible to actually 'being' them. It was really the first time such an authentic blue-collar character was seen on stage and it has remained in the public memory.

SETTING

The Vieux Carré, or French Quarter is an extremely appropriate choice of setting for *A Streetcar Named Desire*. It shows a true picture of where America was heading in the 1940/50s. It is a vibrant city with a mesh of cultures and thriving industry.

Williams gives a pretty accurate picture of what it would be like to live in this town. The Mexican Flower Seller, The Negro Woman, the street vendors all help to give a true atmosphere to the play.

In scene 10 the back wall of the apartment is supposed to disappear to reveal a clear scrim. Behind the scrim we see a prostitute 'rolling' (stealing from) a drunk. This comes as Blanche is desperately trying to contact Shep Huntley because she feels threatened by Stanley. The reality of what is happening outside contrasts deeply with the fantasy world Blanche is retreating to.

EXTENSION OF REALISM

Williams creates on stage a real world and real characters who are fragile and face dilemmas. The way he chooses to explore these characters and this world is not realistic at all. He gives greater depth to them by using expressionistic techniques

Blanche is a classic example of where Williams stretches realism. There are some very real aspects to her life such as the destruction of her family, her sexual indiscretions and her determination to survive. The audience is also faced with a very real dilemma as to how much (if at all) they sympathise with her at various points in the play.

However Blanche is also clearly unbalanced and to truly understand her Williams needed to go beyond a purely realistic character. That is why the audience hears the Varsouviana that constantly plays in her head. It is why there are all the symbolic allusions of light and dark. The audience sees and hears on stage what is going on in Blanche's head.

REALISM/EXPRESSIONISM/SYMBOLISM SUMMARY

REALISM	EXPRESSIONISM	SYMBOLISM
CHARACTERS	**THE OUTWARD EXPRESSION OF BLANCHE'S INNER THOUGHTS**	**DESIRE AND CEMETRIES**
Easily recognisable	Varsouviana	Blanche's fate
Human	Sounds of the city	
ACTION	**STRUCTURE**	**'FOOD AND DRINK**
Focus is on everyday events	The play revolves around 'the spoilt occasion' and can be divided into three acts Act 1-win for Stanley Act 2-win for Blanche Act 3-win for Stanley	Victory and celebration. Whoever has the drink or the food is fortunate

REALISM	EXPRESSIONISM	SYMBOLISM
MORAL DILEMMAS	**LIGHTING**	**ELYSIAN FIELDS**
Does the audience sympathise with Blanche?	Lighting expresses the concept of reality versus illusion	Paradise
LANGUAGE	**LANGUAGE**	**COLOURS**
Working Class	Blanche- poetry	Primary Colours are the truth
SETTING		**'FLOWERS FOR THE DEAD'**
The French Quarter. Where America was heading in 1940/50**s**		Blanche's anxieties and fate

A CONTEMPORARY PRODUCTION

STEFFENWOLF THEATRE 1997 PRODUCTION

This production was considered both an artistic and commercial success. Those involved sought to make a version of *A Streetcar Named Desire* that was wholly their own.

The setting was painted in blacks, browns and greys and lit in yellow tones that made it welcoming and at the same time disconcerting. The essential elements are there just as Williams described them-including the famed staircase.

The jazz music that creates the vibrant New Orleans atmosphere was present-not only during the scenes but in the scene changes. It gradually got more insistent and menacing as the play wore on. Cleverly this suggests that 'apes' and their modern existence are defeating Blanche.

The biggest change was perhaps in characterisation. Stanley is the most difficult character to play well because it is too easy to make him stylised and a caricature. There is also the legacy of Marlon Brando-who played him first on stage and also in the 1951 film, all actors since are inevitably compared to him. Gary Sinise, who played Stanley in this production, did not try to copy Brando but made Stanley wholly his own. He shows more glimpses of Stanley's inner weakness. He is frequently hunched over and rubbing his temples. However he does not shy away from the more violent aspects of Stanley, appearing truly menacing, particularly during the rape scene.

This production also included a few moments that are usually kept off stage. The audience actually sees Stanley hit Stella and her lurching steps across the stage after convey the full impact of such violence. Also after this the audience watches (or is forced to watch?) the very sexual nature of their reconciliation that culminates with Stella straddling her husband's waist as he carries her to their bed. The audience has a new and intimate insight when Stella says, 'there are things that happen between a man and a woman in the dark-that sort of make everything else seem-unimportant.'

This production managed to be original while also capturing William's concerns of capturing conflicting worlds and the spirit of New Orleans in the 1940's.

DIRECTORS COMMENTS

Directors are often the best source of information on how exactly a play works (or doesn't work). The decisions they make say a great deal about the play.

'This is a poetic tragedy. We are shown the final dissolution of a person of worth who once had great potential and who, even as she goes down, has worth exceeding that of the healthy, coarse grained figures who kill her....'
(Elia Kazaan, 1947)

'Stanley's key is his self-absorption; he's the baby who yells when the nipple is pulled from his mouth.'
(Elia Kazaan, 1947)

'It is a real life soap opera.'
(Martie Ramm Fullerton College Theatre Department, 2005 production)

'Williams felt the "look" was particularly important in conveying the poetic and metaphorical meanings of the play.'
(John Rindo, Puget Sound Theatre 2001 Production)

'Blanche arrives and if only she had been given a higher level of kindness, I think there would have been a very different reality that she confronts at the end of the play.'

(Richard Seyd, American Conservatory Theatre 2000
production)

THEATRICAL TECHNIQUES AND LANGUAGE QUESTIONS

❑ Humidity is another important symbol Williams uses. What does it represent and how is it conveyed?

❑ What are the most important elements of the set for this play?

❑ Blanche seems to speak a totally different language to the inhabitants of The French Quarter yet she understands Stanley perfectly well when he asks her if she is going to, 'shack up here'. What does this suggest about Blanche?

❑ Besides defining character and creating atmosphere what role do food, drink and the poker night play in *A Streetcar Named Desire*?

❑ Why does Blanche try to contact Shep Huntley in scene 10?

❑ Tennessee Williams considered other titles for this play including The Moth, The Poker Night, The Primary Colours and Blanche's Chair in the Moon. What is the significance of each of these to the play?

❑ When are the sounds of the train tracks heard during the play? Why are they heard in those moments?

❑ What else does the symbolism of the exterior world invading the interior of the apartment suggest besides Blanche's distress?

❑ What new elements would you incorporate into a contemporary production of *A Streetcar Named Desire*?

CRITIC'S RESPONSES TO *A Streetcar Named Desire*

Considering just how critics have responded to *A Streetcar Named Desire*, after it was written and to various performances of it gives a greater appreciation of just what a classic it is. Also critics often point out what are the essential elements of the play.

'For he (Williams) has not forgotten that human beings are the basic subject of art. Out of poetic imagination and ordinary compassion he has spun a poignant and luminous story.'
(BROOKS ATKINSON, New York Times on 1947 Broadway Production)

'The play balances exaggerated melodrama and irony, never allowing us to feel an emotion about a character or an act without seeing how others feel differently, how other ways of looking at it are possible.'
(RUSS HUNT on Theatre New Brunswick 1994 Production)

'Amy Laxineta imbues Blanche DuBois with appropriate measures of vanity, poetry, sensuality, vulnerability, fading beauty and failing sanity. She eloquently delivers Williams' language with a Southern quaver that charms with its range rather than cloys with sentimentality, making us understand Mitch's infatuation and Stella's indulgences.'

(NANCY CROUSE on Montana Repertory Theatre September 2004 production)

'The archetypal fading Southern belle, Blanche is both a fully realised character and a metaphor for the sensitive spirit, inherently fragile and often bruised by the harsh realities of life.'
(AMANDA HODGES on Lytelton Theatre's October 2004 Production)

'57 years has not tainted the power and majesty of *A Streetcar Named Desire*. It is as relevant today as in 1947 when it was cutting-edge theatre. Actually, I believe this icon has improved with age, a vintage for the soul.'
(TOM WILLIAMS on Raven Theatre's 2000 Production)

MODEL ESSAY

Read carefully the question below and then examine the essay outline on the following pages. Try to develop your essay along these lines and develop strategies to answer questions that are not essay based.

A list of these response types is given at the end of the sample essay. Look at these and you should be familiar with most of them. Try to practice them when you can and develop your writing skills.

Remember that while in this question you asked to refer only to A Streetcar Named Desire in the HSC Drama examination you probably will be required to refer to two texts set for America Drama.

QUESTION

'*A Streetcar Named Desire* examines moral dilemmas that are real, using non-realistic dramatic styles'

Evaluate this statement with examples from the text.

THE ESSAY

The essay has been the subject of numerous texts and you should have the basic form well in hand. As teachers, the point we would emphasise would be to link the paragraphs both to each other and back to your argument (which should directly respond to the question). Of course ensure your argument is logical and sustained.

Make sure you use specific examples and that your quotes are accurate. To ensure that you respond to the question make sure you plan carefully and are sure what relevant point each paragraph is making. It is solid technique to actually 'tie up' each point by explicitly coming back to the question.

When composing an essay the basic conventions of the form are:

- State your argument, outline the points to be addressed and perhaps have a brief definition.

A solid structure for each paragraph is:
- Topic sentence *(the main idea and its link to the previous paragraph/argument)*
- Explanation / discussion of the point including links between texts if applicable.
- Detailed evidence *(Close textual reference- quotes, incidents and technique discussion.)*
- Tie up by restating the point's relevance to argument / question

- Summary of points
- Final sentence that restates your argument

As well as this basic structure you will need to focus on:

Audience – for the essay the audience must be considered formal unless specifically stated otherwise. Therefore your language must reflect the audience. This gives you the opportunity to use the jargon and vocabulary that you have learnt in Drama. For the audience ensure your introduction is clear and has impact. Avoid slang or colloquial language including contractions (like doesn't, eg. etc.).

Purpose – the purpose of the essay is to answer the question given. The examiner evaluates how well you can make an argument and understand the module's issues and its text(s). An essay is solidly structured so its composer can analyse ideas. This is where you earn marks. It does not retell the story or state the obvious.

Communication – Take a few minutes to plan the essay. If you rush into your answer it is almost certain you will not make the most of the time allocated to show all you know about the question. More likely you will include irrelevant details that do not gain you marks but waste your precious time. Remember an essay is formal so **do not** do the following: story-tell, list and number points, misquote, use slang or colloquial language, be vague, use non sentences or fail to address the question.

MODEL ESSAY – *A Streetcar Named Desire*

'*A Streetcar Named Desire* examines moral dilemmas that are real, using non-realistic dramatic styles?'

Evaluate this statement with examples from the text.

A few notes about the question:

- ℘ Remember the actual question is asking you what you have learned about both the moral dilemmas and themes in the play as well as its non-realistic style.

- ℘ The quote that begins the question is more to point you in the right direction.

- ℘ It is important you take note of the ideas the quote raises and check your response does address them.

- ℘ Take care you use the number of texts the examiner asks for. There is no value in writing on more and you will **definitely** be penalised for writing on less. (In drama you will usually be asked to refer to two)

- ℘ You MUST have quotations and textual references that show you have a good knowledge and understanding of your prescribed texts.

© Five Senses Education Pty Ltd

ജ Your response must look at BOTH **WHAT** the text has taught you about realism and expressionism AND **HOW** Williams uses these techniques to convey particular moral dilemmas and issues.

ESSAY RESPONSE

'*A Streetcar Named Desire* examines moral dilemmas that are real, using non-realistic dramatic styles'

Evaluate this statement with examples from the text.

A Streetcar Named Desire presents the story of the decline of a dying civilisation through the story of its protagonist Blanche. To fully convey this decline and to gain an insight into Blanche and the other complex characters in this play the realism of the themes and moral dilemmas they face has to be extended using expressionistic techniques. Lighting, Setting, Sound and even the title of the play become total departures from the loud, colourful and extremely real world of New Orleans and the characters that live there. They help to express issues of sexuality and desire that confront these characters. They also confront an audience who is also forced to decide at different points who they have sympathy for-the illusionist Blanche or her realist brother-in-law Stanley? These concerns not only affected the post World War Two society in which the play was written, but also a contemporary audience.

A Streetcar Named Desire plays like an epic battle. There is a battle between reality and illusion and a battle between old and new America. These battles are represented by the conflict between the southern dame school teacher Blanche Dubois and her brutish plant worker brother-in-law Stanley. This poses a clear problem for an audience trying to decide where our sympathies lie between these characters. We, at times may feel as Blanche does that New Orleans (and America in the 1940's by extension) is a crude, jungle like world and the fantasy of the elegant 'Old South' preferable. At other times we agree with Stanley that the illusionary world Blanche creates is abhorrent when she lies to Mitch, for example, about her age.

Structure is the way Williams shifts the audience's sympathies and forces them to consider which, if any, side we believe. Blanche may seem like an intruder at first. She is critical of 'the dreadful conditions' Stella lives in, mocks Stanley and is generally snobbish. Towards the end we realise just how desperate she is to survive following the many deaths in her family, the suicide of her young husband and her scandalous affairs that forced her out of Laurel. In light of all of this Stanley's treatment seems particularly cruel.

The play is clearly divided into three sections that help to express the battle between Blanche and Stanley. There are eleven scenes occurring chronologically between May and September. There are typically two intermissions. The first act ends at scene 4 when Stella tells Blanche she will not be leaving Stanley. This is a loss for Blanche. The second act ends at scene 6, after Mitch and Blanche's date, where she has clearly won his affections. It is a victory for her. The play concludes with Blanche leaves for the mental institution following Stanley's rape. That is his ultimate victory and her tragic loss. The depressing conclusion the audience is left with is that neither side was a good way forward and clearly there is no place in the America of the 1940's for someone as weak and vulnerable as Blanche.

The characters in this play represent extremely real issues of everyday life. They all face loneliness. Blanche has lost so many she loved. Mitch will soon lose his mother. Stella misses Stanley when he is at work and, 'can hardly stand it when he's away for a night'. It is a strange, new existence they face-Stanley and Mitch because it isn't that long since they have returned from war, Stella because she has let. Perhaps this is why they are described in such animalistic ways. Stanley has 'ape-like' qualities, Mitch dances like a bear and the women chatter like hens.

Desire becomes a problematic emotion for several characters in this play that poses serious moral issues. It is hard to ignore the very sexual aspects of this play conveyed in the story of Alan Grey-the young husband who turned to Blanche for help to cope with his 'degenerate' (as it was considered then) homosexual behaviour and was shunned instead. There is also Blanche's unsavoury relations with many strangers and even students and ultimately her rape by Stanley in scene 10. While Blanche is contemptuous of the crudity and violence of Stanley and Stella's lovemaking the audience is made to also feel uncomfortable with Blanche's indiscretions. Blanche suggests that 'the opposite of death is desire' but it is the way these various characters handle it that poses such a dilemma-not just for them but for the audience watching.

Stanley is very real character who poses a dilemma for the audience. What exactly is his reason for destroying Blanche? At first he seems practical. Stanley's investigations into Blanche's recent history begin because he is worried he and Stella have been swindled out of some money from the sale of Belle Reve, and as he says, 'I don't like to be swindled.' He cannot stand to be fooled. When he finds out the truth he is motivated by clear intentions to bring everything out into the open. This is understandable especially as his war-buddy Mitch is involved with Blanche and he doesn't want to see him hurt, he tries to explain to Stella that, 'I'd have that on my conscience the rest of my life if I knew all that stuff and let my best friend get caught!' But perhaps there is selfishness too, as he does not want his relationship with Stella ruined. Blanche has a hold over Stella as she reminds her of their previous glamorous life and points out how 'common' Stanley is. There is also the possibility that he wanted Mitch out of the picture so he could keep the horrible 'date' he believes he and Blanche had from the beginning. Towards the end it also seems pure vindictiveness because he cannot stand Blanche's insults. The audience is left to way up the possibility that it is for one, some or all of these reasons Stanley destroys Blanche by raping her.

Lighting is used to convey the reality that invades the illusion created by Blanche. Blanche lives in a world of make believe to hide from the past and the deaths of her family and young husband. To relive what she perceives as the glorious experience of her youth at her beloved Belle Reve she constantly hides from light to fool herself (and others) into thinking she's younger. The covering of the 'naked light bulb' that so disgusts her becomes symbolic of Blanche's desire to not face reality. She justifies it as 'a little magic to in order to pay for one night's shelter.' This comment makes the audience aware of the deeper implications of Blanche's actions. She can't accept everything that has happened to her and she can't be alone-she needs to desired and feels she has to trick men to achieve this.

Blanche's aversion to light is contrasted with the staunch realist Stanley. Stanley doesn't cover light bulbs with paper lanterns he smashes them. He cannot stand to be lied to, and searches until he finds the truth about Blanche's recent indiscretions. Ultimately the reality of Stanley's post war world in The French Quarter achieves victory over Blanche because she is clinging to something that simply does not exist any more.

The sounds of the past and of the city haunt Blanche and give the audience some indication of her growing mental instability. The repetition of the waltz music that was playing the night Alan Grey killed himself, followed by a gunshot represents Blanche's guilt over her naïve insensitivity.

Train noises, as well as representing the city, give an indication of Blanche's instability as the audience if never really sure, especially towards the end, whether any one else on stage can hear these noises. They suggest that the exterior world of New Orleans is invading Blanche's internal one. Another example of this is the calls of the Mexican woman, 'flowers for the dead.' This symbolises the fate of Blanche but also her descent into madness the audience again isn't sure if the woman is real. To gain a clearer insight into the Blanche's mind Williams had to use these non-realistic techniques. Therefore the audience does not just see Blanche's reaction to her internal turmoil, it is given outward representation on stage.

The setting of the play is incredibly realistic. Great detail is given in the production notes to describe the French Quarter and how it is, '*cramped and bustling with life.*' Characters interact with Stanley and Stella's apartment as people do in real life. Food is eaten; messes are made and cleaned up. Willliams goes beyond this however. He needs the audience to understand the spirit of the place and how much it conflicts with Blanche. That is why the music of the blue piano is used to establish the mood of New Orleans. The set also changes in scene 10 (the rape scene). The directions indicate that the back wall of the apartment is to become a transparent scrim and the audience sees a prostitute stealing from a drunk. Not only does this give the audience the idea of the 'mean streets' outside it also suggests reality is overcoming Blanche as Stanley is attacking her. Stanley and the harsh 'New America' defeat Blanche.

The title of the play at first appears realistic. It is the name of the streetcar, 'that bangs up one old street and down another' and transports Blanche to Stella and Stanley's home. It also becomes symbolic of Blanche's fortune. She tells us that 'they told me to take a streetcar named Desire, and then transfer to one called Cemeteries and ride six blocks and get off at-Elysian Fields!' Blanche's desire for intimacies with strangers was what forced out of her hometown and into staying with Stella and Stanley. They live in Elysian Fields, or paradise. Because paradise was only created for two it will mean the destruction of Blanche and a 'transfer to cemeteries' is inevitable.

It is true that *A Streetcar Named Desire* examines moral dilemmas that are real but using non-realistic or expressionistic techniques. Realism conveys real feelings and emotions to a point but to truly understand the psychology of the characters in this play, particularly the complex Blanche, and the dilemmas they (and us as an audience) face realism must be extended through symbolism and expressionistic techniques.

ESSAY QUESTIONS

❏ 'The use of expressionistic and symbolist techniques to extend realism in America drama makes these plays still relevant to contemporary society.'

Evaluate this statement in relation to the ways in which *A Streetcar Named Desire* might be produced on a contemporary stage

❏ How did Tennessee Williams use the style and conventions of theatre to make audiences look at their society in different ways?

❏ 'The style of a play says a lot about the time it was written and what societies concerns were'

Discuss in relation to *A Streetcar Named Desire.*

❑ '*And so it was I entered the broken world*

    To trace the visionary company of love, its voice

    An instant in the wind (I know not whither hurled)

    But not for long to hold each desperate choice'

                    (HART CRANE *The Broken Tower*)

Williams includes this quote as a preface to *A Streetcar Named Desire*. What does it express about his characters and concerns? How does he choose to convey this on stage?

❑ How does Tennessee William use expressionist, symbolist and realist techniques to explore American society post World War Two?

❑ '*For he (Williams) has not forgotten that human beings are the basic subject of art.'*

What does *A Streetcar Named Desire* express about human beings? How is it expressed?